A BAKER'S DOZEN

CLASSROOM ENSEMBLES FOR VOICES, RECORDERS, AND ORFF INSTRUMENTS

JANE FRAZEE   ✳   ARVIDA STEEN

ART WORK: MARSHALL FERSTER

INTRODUCTION

The musical recipes contained in this collection have been tested and approved by children.

An appropriate music making diet for children consists of a variety of poems, songs, and dances. In this book students are encouraged to improvise with basic musical ingredients: rhythm, melody, harmony, form, and tone color to make an infinite variety of original confections. The master chef, the teacher, encourages innovative ways to use the materials and equipment at hand.

The proof of the pudding will be the delight and satisfaction which children feel as they contribute to their musical ensembles.

TABLE OF CONTENTS

TIPS FOR THE MASTER CHEF

1. Always play and sing at the same time.

2. Encourage alternation of mallets from the beginning.

3. Stems pointing down in the score indicate left-hand mallet, stems pointing up indicate right-hand mallet.

4. A star in the score refers to improvisation.

5. Body ostinato parts are notated on a four-line staff.

6. Patschen ostinato parts are notated on a two-line staff. Stems pointing down indicate left-hand movement, stems pointing up indicate right-hand.

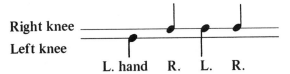

7. The hand staff is used for learning note names to be applied to instrumental parts. The hand signals are used for learning syllables, which usually apply to a vocal part.

8. Teach song material using rote or note approach, as preferred.

9. Teach all the students all the parts.

10. Activities for each song are not always listed sequentially.

11. Select as few or as many suggested activities as are appropriate for the lesson.

12. Activities may be repeated, giving opportunities for exchanging singing, playing, and movement experiences.

 Musical elements explored in each lesson may lead to a variety of meaningful listening activities.

TERMS FOR THE MASTER CHEF

Augmentation: To double time values

Bordun: A drone bass, consisting of the first and fifth tones of the scale

Canon: The imitation of a melodic or rhythmic theme by one or more voices starting at successively later points

Hand signals: Hand movements denoting tone syllables

Hand staff: Fingers representing ledger lines of staff

Improvisation: To invent without preparation

Mirror movement: To reflect another person's movement

Motive: A fragment of a melodic or rhythmic theme

Ostinato: A repeated rhythmic or melodic pattern

Patschen: Thigh slapping

Pentachord: The first five tones of the diatonic scale

Pentatonic: A five-tone scale which has no semitones

Retrograde: Backward reading of a pattern

Rondo: A composition having a refrain that occurs at least three times between contrasting material

Tremolo: A rapid alternation of one or two tones

Instrumental Abbreviations

SG:	Soprano glockenspiel		BM:	Bass metallophone
AG:	Alto glockenspiel		FC:	Finger cymbals
SX:	Soprano xylophone		HD:	Hand drum
AX:	Alto xylophone		WB:	Woodblocks
BX:	Bass xylophone		T:	Triangle
SM:	Soprano metallophone		BD:	Bongo drum
AM:	Alto metallophone		TB:	Temple blocks

CINDERELLA

1. Say: Cinderella dress'd in yella
            Went downstairs to kiss her fella

   Clap pulse lightly at the same time. Try clapping every other beat.

2. Sing S M S and S L S melodic patterns with hand signals.

3. Students read the melodic outline with syllables from notation:

4. Sing song as written in the score, pointing to the melodic outline on board or chart. Can a student lead the singing?

5. Isolate S M S pattern from melodic outline by singing letter names of the first three notes. Play this pattern on a variety of instruments.

6. Isolate and play S L S pattern as in Step 5 above.

7. Sing the song, patschen every other beat with both hands simultaneously. Transfer patschen pattern to BX, playing the simple bordun (F and C).

8. Students patschen pulse, alternating hands while they sing. Divide into two groups. Patschen one-measure pattern alternating between the groups while singing.

9. Transfer patschen pattern to xylophones, SX answering AX. (See score.)

10. Play and sing the first four bars of Cinderella. Voices add the next phrase, "how many kisses did she get," on the syllable sol. Be sure accompaniment stops at the end of the fourth bar!

11. HD maintains pulse for eight additional beats while WB improvises the number of Cinderella's kisses. Can students begin to use silences and eighth notes in their improvisations?

12. Form circle around WB and HD players. Holding hands and singing, walk four steps toward center of the circle, then take four steps back. Drop hands and shout the number of kisses after WB improvisation. New players go to center of the circle and dance begins again.

 Sing and play "Cinderella" in C pentatonic.

CINDERELLA

Cin - der - el - la,   dressed in   yel - la,   went down- stairs   to   kiss   her   fel - la.

How ma-ny kis-ses   did she get ?

Improvisation

RAIN DANCE

1. Say:

   Use "Come good rain" as a spoken ostinato for the first line of the poem.

2. Teach Rain Dance song.

3. Sing the song and patschen pulse. Don't forget to alternate hands!

4. Sing the song while BX plays the pulse (alternating mallets) on E to establish the tonal center.

5. Outline the melody by singing note names in quarter notes from hand staff.

6. Try playing the melody outline on a variety of instruments.

7. Patschen ♩ ♪ ♩ ♪ ♩ ♩ ♩ ♪ with both hands simultaneously. Half the group continues this pattern while other half sings. Reverse. All then sing and patschen at the same time.

8. Transfer patschen pattern to AX. Play pattern on E and B together until well established. Then encourage student to alter part as written in the score.

9. Clap, from notation, the rhythm patterns ♩ ♪♪ :‖ and ♪♪ ♪♪ :‖ . HD plays ♩ ♪♪ :‖ , jingles answer ♪♪ ♪♪:‖ . Can jingles play the answer only when HD continues an ostinato? (See score.)

10. Play BX, AX, AM, and percussion while singing.

11. Try an eight beat SG improvisation, followed by an eight beat AG improvisation using notes from melody outline. Try the B part on piano or tympani.

12. Form a snake dance line. Walk and bend knee (dip) on first of every four beats. Transfer to AM. Group reverses direction and the last person becomes the new leader for B improvisation section. On return to A change to original direction and a few students chant (or sing on E) "Come good rain" while others sing the melody.

 Try an authentic Indian dance step. Right toe-heel, left toe-heel in steady pulse in a large circle while singing.

RAIN DANCE

1. Come a _ gain, Come a _ gain, Come, good rain,
2. Come a - gain, Come a - gain, Come, good rain,

Fall up _ on the moun _ tains, and on the plain.
Wa - ter for the ri - ver, and for the grain.

*Improvisation

AG*

D.C. al Fine

SchBk 9058

LULLABY

1. Share this poem with the class:

   Round round, fat and round

   So many things in the world are round.

2. Class says first line, followed by eight beats for individual student responses.

   Example: Class: Round round, fat and round

   Solo: Circle, orange, great big hole!

   Repeat several times with new responses, ending with the second line of poem.

3. BX or BM plays "round round" (♩ ♩) with right mallet, left mallet plays only first pulse. Class imitates the same part in patschen.

4. Teacher plays AG mallet movement in air. Students mirror while chanting "fat and round." Can they sing this pattern in syllables?

5. Notate the rhythm of "fat and round" in quarter notes. Can students notate this rhythm in half notes? The half note rhythm becomes the AM part. Play AG and AM together.

6. Teacher sings the song with the orchestral accompaniment and students echo.

7. When song is familiar, students notate it, one measure at a time.

8. Using student notation, sing the melody backwards.

9. For improvisation section, BX or BM plays "round round, fat and round" (♩ ♩ ♩ ♩ ♩) in simple bordun (D and A) while class hums new melodies based on material from song. One student may wish to sing his melody on "loo" while others hum.

10. Perform the Lullaby A A B B.

11. Step rhythm of poem "round round, fat and round." Now step rhythm of poem and sing the song.

12. Can someone play the melody on a xylophone? Perform the Lullaby as an orchestral piece, AX playing song melody. Add movement from number 11.

 Can students play the first three measures of the AG part in retrograde?

LULLABY

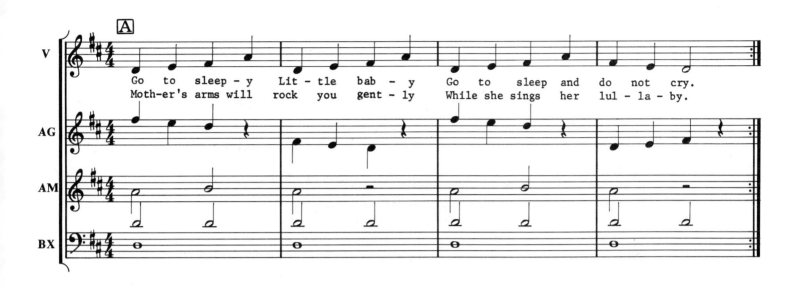

Go to sleep - y   Lit - tle   bab - y   Go to   sleep and   do   not   cry.
Moth-er's arms will   rock   you   gent - ly   While she sings   her   lul - la - by.

*Voices improvise on "nnn."

Fine

I WANT TO RISE

1. Students learn song as they patschen the pulse.

2. Students sing the song and clap the first pulse of each phrase. Repeat the song, clapping at the beginning and end of each phrase. Transfer this pattern to AG.

3. Walk pulse, changing directions at the beginning of each phrase, clapping as before.

4. Patschen pulse:  Transfer to AX.

5. Students walk:

    step together step together   step step step together

    Can they clap each time they step forward? Transfer clapped pattern to BX.

6. Say "Early morn" (♩ ♩ ♩ ♩) then "Rise in the morn" (♩ ♫ ♩ ♩). Students notate these patterns.

7. Students snap ♩ ♩ ♩ ♩ then clap ♩ ♫ ♩ ♩ Transfer the first pattern to FC, the second to HD. (See score.)

8. Sing song with orchestration.

9. Arrange instruments in F pentatonic. Four students improvise eight-beat melodic phrases on SG or AG. Try to incorporate ♩ ♩ ♩ ♩ and ♩ ♫ ♩ ♩ into the improvisation. BX plays the note F using AX rhythm pattern from above.

10. Using the improvisation as a B section, sing and play in a three-part form.

11. Make a simple circle dance. Outside circle steps AX rhythm pattern clockwise and inside circle steps BX rhythm pattern counterclockwise. Sing, dance A section, patschen pulse during B section. Don't forget to add the orchestra!

12. Students will enjoy introducing the song with waking up movements.

 Can you think of ways to use contrasting instrumental colors to expand this form into a rondo?

I WANT TO RISE

I want to rise in the ear-ly morn, I want to rise in the ear-ly morn.

I want to rise in the ear-ly morn, and I'll ne-ver sleep late an-y more.

* Improvisation

DOWN THE ROAD

1. Teach the melodic motives M R D and S₁L₁ D using hand signals. Students notate these patterns.

2. Students clap ♩ ♩ ♩ ￼ from notation. Change first quarter to an eighth note. Students decide how to alter the second note to accommodate this change.

3. Clap ♩ ♩ ♩ ￼ and ♪ ♩. ♩ ￼ , alternating several times. Sing these rhythms using melodic motives from number 1.

4. Teacher sings song. Can students identify the familiar rhythmic and melodic motives?

5. Students sing song, clapping syncopated motive when it occurs.

6. Walk quarter notes while snapping half notes. Transfer snapped half note pattern to BX, alternating mallets each measure. Now sing the song, play, walk, and snap.

7. Continue walking quarters and clap ♩ ￼ ♩ ♩ . Stop walking, transfer to patschen:

   , then to two SX. Add BX, AX, and sing.

8. Sing the song, clapping ♪ ♩. ♩ ￼ each time you sing "road." Transfer this part to the triangle.

9. Students make several groups of two lines, partners facing one another. Take three steps forward, clapping partner's hands on fourth beat. Walk backward next three beats, clapping your own hands on fourth beat. During next eight beat phrase, head couple joins hands to make an arch. Rear couple walks "down the road" formed by the two lines and through the arch. They now become the head couple. This dance is adapted from the Virginia Reel.

10. Sing, play and dance "Down the Road."

11. For an improvisation, establish WB and FC ostinati from score. Using rhythmic motives from the song, experiment with the colors of bongo drum or temple blocks in creating a percussion improvisation. This new material may be used as an introduction, interlude, or code.

12. Try performing "Down the Road" using additive orchestration. One instrument is added each time the song is repeated, as indicated in the score.

Say the poem: The ants walk under the giant feet
                  Of the elephants, when they go to eat.

Experiment with percussion instruments to represent ants and elephants walking "down the road."

DOWN THE ROAD

SIOUX INDIAN LULLABY

1. Let's play a change game with meter. Play, imitating teacher:
   Repeat several times.
   When pattern is secure change to:

   Continue playing patterns, choosing a magic word to signal meter changes.

2. Walk triple pulse, clapping on the first beat. Transfer clapped beats to finger cymbals.
   Clap: ♫ ♫ ♩ . Transfer to HD.

3. Teach the first phrase of the song with syllables beginning on la. Sing and play with percussion accompaniment.

4. Notate the first phrase of the song.

5. Walk ♩ ♩ and sing melody. BX plays this ostinato.

6. Students mirror AX mallet movement from teacher's example in air. Transfer to instrument. Sing and play all parts.

7. Echo sing $\frac{4}{4}$ section while stepping half notes. Add AM. Add tremolo on one AG. Sing and play first two sections.

8. Each student walks BX, then AM rhythms in his own space accompanied by BX and AM. Can students notate these rhythm patterns?

9. Use rhythms from BX and AM for a partner dance. Face partner, arms folded in front of chest moving backward: step together step together, and forward: step together step together. Join hands, pulling away from one another on first half note, relaxing on the second during the $\frac{4}{4}$ section.

10. Adding recorder and percussion, sing, play and dance.

11. Say: $\frac{3}{4}$ ♩ ♩ ♩ ♩
    Soft wind, Soft wind

    $\frac{4}{4}$ ♩ ♩ ♩   ♫ ♫ ♩ ♩
    Sing for me, Sing a song for me.

12. Improvise color atmospheres for "soft wind" $(\frac{3}{4})$ contrasted with "sing for me" $(\frac{4}{4})$. Explore the sound possibilities of your classroom environment.

   Try singing the song in canon with recorder. Recorder enters one measure after the voices begin.

SIOUX INDIAN LULLABY

Na-na-na sleep my small one, Na-na-na, sleep my small one. Mo-ther is near you.

Noth-ing will harm you Na-na-na, sleep my small one. (Recorder only)_____

HERE STANDS A REDBIRD

1. Using a blackboard or overhead, sing these melodic motives from the song:

2. Play a game with motives. Students sing as teacher calls motive numbers. Example: 21 means sing two, then one. Students will enjoy inventing new combinations.

3. Sing AM part from score using letter names. Students play AM phrase on various instruments.

4. Teach the first two phrases of the song. Compare first measure of the voice line with the AM part. Sing and play the first two phrases.

5. Clap, then patschen the BX rhythm (𝅗𝅥. 𝅘𝅥) with both hands, moving left hand out on the fourth beat. Play pattern on BX. Sing and play all parts.

6. Teach last phrase of song. Is it like the first two phrases?

7. Clap ♩ ♪ ♩ ♪ ♩ ♩ 𝄾 from notation. Does this sound like "tra la la la la" from the song? Correct the written notation and clap it. Then clap ♪. ♫ ♪. ♫ ♩ ♩ ♪. ♫ ♪. ♫ ♪ Play on AG while singing last phrase. (See score.)

   Patschen [musical notation] . Transfer to AX. Sing and play third phrase.

8. Sing and play entire song. What is the form of this song?

9. While stepping pulse class reads: The owl did hoot,
                                         The birds they sang,
                                         And through the woods the music rang.

   Compare phrase lengths of the poem with phrase lengths of the song.

10. Play the rhythm of each of the three phrases of the poem on a different percussion instrument.

11. Try this simple dance as you sing the song. Form groups of three holding hands throughout the song. Skip first phrase clockwise, second phrase counterclockwise. On the last phrase leader goes out through the window formed by the other partners' hands, turning the circle inside out. While percussionists play poem as in number 10 leader walks backward, pulling partners in through the window. Repeat the dance twice giving each student an opportunity to lead.

12. Small groups create a rhythmic improvisation in A A B form using body sounds. Students select phrase length. However, the second A will be an echo of the first; B equals the two A's in length. Invite each group to share its piece with the class.

    Do you know other songs in A A B form?

HERE STANDS A RED BIRD

Here stands a red bird, Tra - la-la - la-la. Here stands a red bird, Tra-la-la - la-la.

Rice, su-gar and tea.

2. Make a pret-ty mo-tion, Tra-la-la-la-la. Rice, su-gar and tea.

From the Frank C. Brown Collection Vol. III; Folk Songs of North Carolina
© 1952. Duke University Press, Newman Ivey White, General Editor.

FROG IN A BOG

1. Sing the pentachord based on F using syllables, then letter names on a hand staff. Notate and play ascending and descending.

2. Sing syllables of pentachord ascending and descending in two-part canon at the time interval of two beats.

3. Can students sing the pentachord in half notes as the teacher sings the song? Learn the A section of the song.

4. Play melodic line in steady quarter notes on AG while students sing. Invert this line, playing each note twice, creating the AG part.

5. Play a broken simple bordun (F, C) on BX while singing and playing AG. Remedy the resulting dissonance by changing the bass line to root of V. (See score.)

6. Echo clap and notate ♪♩♪♪♩ ♩ ♪♪♪♪ ♩ ⸰ . Transfer to AX.

7. Teach "better go round," filling the rests in the vocal line by clapping ♪♪♩ . AX plays this response while other instruments play ♩ ♩ .

8. Sing the song in canon with accompaniment.

9. Play with the words "better go round." Make word phrases using the two rhythmic values and rests. Example: "Round, round, round, better go round, round." (♩ ♩ ♩ ♩♪♪♩ ♩ ⸰ ⸰ ♩)

10. Transfer this rhythmic material to four percussion instruments to improvise a 16 bar B section.

11. Form several groups of two lines facing each other with two or three partners in each line (four or six people). The lines walk forward stepping four half notes while singing, then pivoting and returning on the next four half notes. Face partner, join hands, and "wring the dishrag" (turning inside and out) after singing each "better go round." Try this in canon, line one beginning dance while singing, line two beginning on third half note.

12. After singing and dancing in canon, take a little walk with your partner wherever you like, accompanied by the percussion improvisation. The trick is to form one large circle by the end of the sixteen bar section. Sing song again in unison, walking around the circle, and wringing the dishrag with your partner as you did before.

 The students might enjoy singing "The Frog in a Bog" tune in inversion.

THE FROG IN THE BOG

A JOYFUL NOISE

1. Learn the song.

2. Clap, then step in circle:  . When it is well established add song.

3. Form two concentric circles, boys outside and girls inside facing each other, hands on hips. Boys and girls exchange places on phrase 1, return on phrase 2.

    R L R   Turn   Together   L R L   Turn   Together

    Pass right shoulders on first exchange, left on return. Move and sing phrases one and two.

4. While singing the last phrase, walk the pattern (number 2 above) twice in opposite directions in the circle to find a new partner. Sing the song adding movement patterns in sequence.

5. Teach bass line by phrases using hand staff, singing letter names. Students play bass line while singing song; note the lengthened third phrase.

6. Teach first two measures of AG part using hand staff singing lower voice alone. Play it together with BX. Now play AG part in thirds as written; add BX.

7. Notate the first two measures of BX and AG parts.

8. Teach last two measures of third phrase of AG as an inversion of first measure. Play BX, AG, and sing melody.

9. Clap WB part. After it has been mastered, try clapping it while singing. Add WB to the orchestration and perform.

10. Think of some happy words to introduce the song. Chant "happy day" (♩ ♩ o) as an ostinato. Several students, in turn, speak their happy words during the last measure of the ostinato. Example:

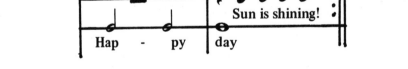

    Hap - py | day   Sun is shining!

11. Sing, play, and dance, adding the tambourine as indicated. Don't forget the introduction!

12. Build the tonic, sub-dominant, and dominant chords in C major. Can students find these chords in the first two measures of the song previously notated?

Can students discover the reason for the bass line change in the last two measures?

A JOYFUL NOISE

Make a joy-ful noise to-ge-ther, with all the earth your mu-sic___play.

Come, re-joice and sing___ to-ge-ther this___ hap - py day!

DORIAN CANON

1. Walk quarter notes. Change direction at signal. Experiment with different phrase lengths, finally establishing eight beat phrases. Walk ♩ , clap ♫♩ . Change direction and clap 𝅗𝅥 while walking quarter notes.

2. Say the poem: The long brown path before me,
                             Leading wherever I choose.

3. Clap the rhythm of the poem in canon at two-bar intervals. Try a three-part and a four-part canon using different body sounds for each part.

4. Speak the poem in unison with a BX tremolo accompaniment on D.

5. Step the rhythm of the poem in unison, then in canon.

6. Student plays C major scale on an instrument of his choice. Suggest he play the same scale beginning on D. Identify the dorian scale and invite class to sing letter names while the student plays.

7. Teach opening six-note motive of the song with syllables beginning on "re" and write it. Learn the remaining part of the phrase. Sing the song in unison, then in canon.

8. Clap ♩ ♩ ♫♩ ♩ . Transfer to BX.

9. Patschen ♩ ♫♩ ♩ 𝄾 defining the rest by moving arms out (see SX, SM in score). Sing, using this pattern as a rhythmic ostinato. Patschen ♩ ♩ ♩ 𝄾 while singing melody (AX, AM in score).

10. Divide the class in two parts. Part 1 sings melody with SX, SM, BX. Sing Part 2 with AX and AM. Sing and play all parts in canon.

11. Two melodic instruments improvise in dorian mode on rhythm of the poem in canon at two bar intervals over a BX tremolo on D.

12. Class determines order of the sections of the composition, arranging the material as they choose. One possibility: poem, followed by improvisation, then song. Movement may be adapted from Step 5.

 Try the Dorian Canon in compound duple meter. Can class sing the melody in D major?

DORIAN CANON

Text from Up the Windy Hill by Aileen Fisher. Used by permission.

CORINNA

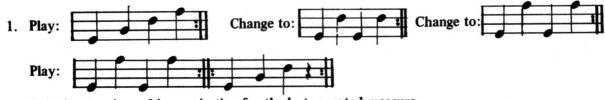

1. Play: Change to: Change to:

   Play:

   Substitute a clapped improvisation for the last repeated measure.

2. Move in any direction on [musical notation] . Improvise free movement in place for next two measures. Repeat several times, changing directions for each four-measure phrase.

3. Add snare or bongo drum playing [musical notation] while students continue movement activity.

4. Teach the song. Drum continues pattern starting on the second measure while class sings.

5. The BX part outlines a typical 12-bar blues progression: 4 bars I, 2 bars IV, 2 bars I, 2 bars V, 2 bars I. Try giving all students an opportunity to play the BX part on an instrument.

6. Notate the bass line, indicating chord changes.

7. Say, "Corinna's gone." ([musical notation]). Clap the rhythm. Divide the class. One group sings the song, the other claps this pattern as an ostinato beginning on the second measure. Repeat, changing parts. Clapping and singing at the same time provides an extra challenge.

8. Play the rhythm pattern "Corinna's gone" in thirds on AX (see score). Note the ascending stepward movement on syllable "na's." Move pattern up one step from tonic for IV, down one step from tonic for V.

9. Sing the song with the orchestration. Don't forget the drum part! Some students may wish to move as in Step 2.

10. Try a talking blues: If you want to get to Heaven let me tell you what to do,
    Gotta grease your feet in mutton stew,
    Slide right out of the Devil's hand
    Ooze over in the promised land
    Take it easy, ...go greasy.

    Say it again, adding bass and percussion. Now make your own talking blues.

11. Talking blues can be used with "Corinna" as a B section of a three-part form.

12. Some students may wish to try "scat" singing (vocal improvisation) when the drummer improvises.

    Try the 12-bar blues pattern in another key.

CORINNA

Co-rin'-na, Co-rin - na, _____ where you been so long? _____

_____ Co-rin-na, Co-rin - na, _____ where you been so long? _____

_____ Ain't had no lov - ing _____ since you been gone.

* Snare drum improvisation

2. Co-rin-na, Co-rin-na, far a-cross the sea (repeat)
She don't write let-ters, don't care for me.

LA RASPA

1. After students have learned the melody (Voice 2 in the score) they will be able to clap melodic rhythm. Can they notate this?

2. Fill the space in the melodic rhythm with the response "Ole." As one section of class claps melodic rhythm, another responds clapping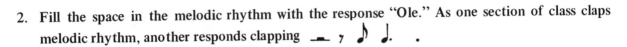

3. Clap a new pattern ♪. ♫ ♪ ♩ ♪. ♫ ♪ ♩ as you sing.

4. Patschen ♩. ♪ ♪ :‖ as you sing. Transfer to BX, using measure one as ostinato for whole song.

5. Did you like the sound? Try again, asking class to clap when they feel the chord should change. BX then plays score as written.

6. Add glockenspiel part to outline chords.

7. Patchen sixteenth notes with both hands. Play sixteenth notes (AX) in thirds, moving both hands down one step each time chord change in BX is heard.

8. Add Voice 1, add instruments, and perform.

9. A rondo form can result from improvised percussion sections contrasted with the song. Try new combinations of rhythmic motives from the song using typical Spanish instruments. The maracas should be played (against palm or thigh) during each improvisation.

10. A simplification of the rhythm of the BX part can make a Latin-like dance. Boys and girls, hands on hips, face each other in two concentric circles and step sideways ♩. ♫ ♩ ♩ ⅟ . (Circles moving in opposite directions will result.) Step the pulse, turning clockwise in place and changing direction after two measures, during improvisations.

11. Make a spoken orchestration with Spanish words that students know. A rondo might be created by contrasting these words with: Con el vito, vito, vito,
                                                                                            Con el vito, vito, va!

12. Clap ♩ ♩ ♩ ♩ ♩ ♩ ♩ ♩ with accents indicated. Try various ways of notating this accent rhythm. For example, see cowbell part.

 Experiment with percussion color adding Spanish instruments to the spoken orchestration. Rhythms may be borrowed from the song, or new ones invented.

LA RASPA

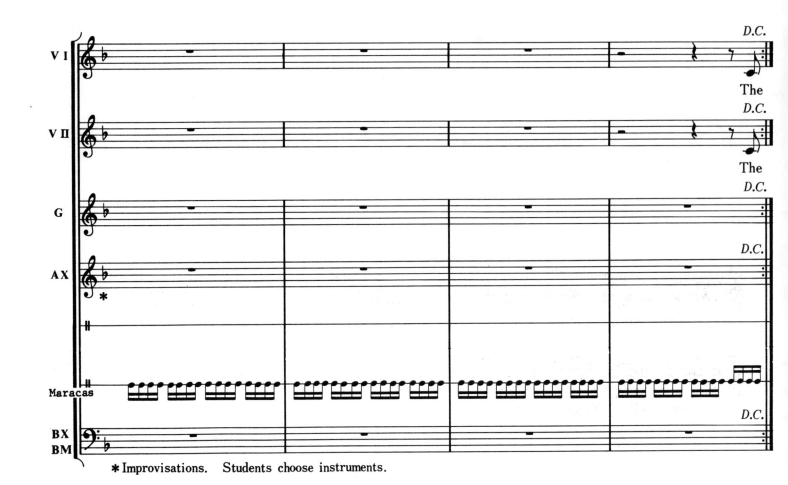

*Improvisations. Students choose instruments.

SING !

Sing and___ re - joice!   **2.** Sing___ and___ re - joice!

3. Let all___ things___ li - ving now sing and re - joice!   **4.**